Shema

שְׁמַע

Jennifer Betham-Lang

Revital Weinstein

langbookpublishing.com

Cover design by Blair McLean

Hebrew translation by Revital Weinstein

National Library of New Zealand Cataloguing-in-Publication Data

Lang Book Publishing 2014

ISBN-13:

978-0-9941117-5-3 Paperback

Published in New Zealand

Shema

שְׁמַע

Designed by Jennifer Betham-Lang
and Revital Weinstein

Deuteronomy 6:4-9

שְׁמַע יִשְׂרָאֵל יְיָ אֱלֹהֵינוּ יְיָ אֶחָד

Sh'ma Yis'ra'eil Adonai Eloheinu Adonai echad.

Hear, Israel, the Lord is our God, the Lord is One.

Previous Page:

Sh'ma Yis'ra'eil Adonai Eloheinu Adonai echad.

Hear, Israel, the Lord is our God, the Lord is One.

בָּרוּךְ שֵׁם כְּבוֹד מַלְכוּתוֹ לְעוֹלָם וָעֶד

Barukh sheim k'vod malkhuto l'olam va'ed.

Blessed be the Name of His glorious kingdom for ever and ever.

Previous Page:

*Barukh sheim k'vod malkhuto l'olam va'ed.

*Blessed be the Name of His glorious kingdom for ever and ever.

וְאָהַבְתָּ אֵת יְיָ אֱלֹהֶיךָ בְּכָל לְבָבְךָ וּבְכָל נַפְשְׁךָ וּבְכָל מְאֹדֶךָ

V'ahav'ta eit Adonai Elohekha b'khol l'vav'kha uv'khol naf'sh'kha uv'khol m'odekha.

And you shall love the Lord your God with all your heart and with all your soul and with all your might.

Previous Page:

V'ahav'ta eit Adonai Elohekha b'khol l'vav'kha uv'khol naf'sh'kha uv'khol m'odekha.

And you shall love the Lord your God with all your heart and with all your soul and with all your might.

וְהָיוּ הַדְּבָרִים הָאֵלֶּה אֲשֶׁר אָנֹכִי מְצַוְּךָ הַיּוֹם עַל לְבָבֶךָ

V'hayu had'varim ha'eileh asher anokhi m'tzav'kha hayom al l'vavekha.

And these words that I command you today shall be in your heart.

Previous Page:

V'hayu had'varim ha'elleh asher anokhi m'tzav'kha hayom al l'vavekha.

And these words that I command you today shall be in your heart.of them.

וְשִׁנַּנְתָּם לְבָנֶיךָ וְדִבַּרְתָּ בָּם

V'shinan'tam l'vanekha v'dibar'ta bam

And you shall teach them diligently to your children, and you shall speak of them.

Previous Page:

V'shinan'tam l'vanekha v'dibar'ta bam

And you shall teach them diligently to your children, and you shall speak of them.

וְהָיוּ הַדְּבָרִים הָאֵלֶּה אֲשֶׁר אָנֹכִי מְצַוְּךָ הַיּוֹם עַל לְבָבֶךָ

V'hayu had'varim ha'eileh asher anokhi m'tzav'kha hayom al l'vavekha.

And these words that I command you today shall be in your heart.

Previous Page:

V'hayu had'varim ha'elleh asher anokhi m'tzav'kha hayom al l'vavekha.

And these words that I command you today shall be in your heart.of them.

בְּשִׁבְתְּךָ בְּבֵיתֶךָ וּבְלֶכְתְּךָ בַדֶּרֶךְ וּבְשָׁכְבְּךָ וּבְקוּמֶךָ

b'shiv't'kha b'veitekha uv'lekh't'kha vaderekh uv'shakh'b'kha uv'kumekha

When you sit at home, and when you walk along the way, and when you lie down and when you rise up.

Previous Page:

b'shiv't'kha b'veitekha uv'lekh't'kha vaderekh uv'shakh'b'kha uv'kumekha

When you sit at home, and when you walk along the way, and when you lie down and when you rise up.

וּקְשַׁרְתָּם לְאוֹת עַל יָדֶךָ וְהָיוּ לְטֹטָפֹת בֵּין עֵינֶיךָ

Uk'shar'tam l'ot al yadekha v'hayu l'totafot bein einekha.

And you shall bind them as a sign on your hand, and they shall be for frontlets between your eyes.

Previous Page:

Uk'shar'tam l'ot al yadekha v'hayu l'totafot bein einekha.

And you shall bind them as a sign on your hand, and they shall be for frontlets between your eyes.

וּכְתַבְתָּם עַל מְזֻזוֹת בֵּיתֶךָ וּבִשְׁעָרֶיךָ

Ukh'tav'tam al m'zuzot beitekha uvish'arekha.

And you shall write them on the doorposts of your house and on your gates.

Previous Page:

Ukh'tav'tam al m'zuzot beitekha uvish'arekha.

And you shall write them on the doorposts of your house and on your gates.

Deuteronomy 11:13-21

וְהָיָה אִם שָׁמֹעַ תִּשְׁמְעוּ אֶל מִצְוֹתַי

V'hayah im shamo'a tish'm'u el mitz'votai

And it shall come to pass if you surely listen to the commandments.

Previous Page:

V'hayah im shamo'a tish'm'u el mitz'votai

And it shall come to pass if you surely listen to the commandments.

אֲשֶׁר אָנֹכִי מְצַוֶּה אֶתְכֶם הַיּוֹם

Asher anokhi m'tzaveh et'khem hayom

That I command you today.

Previous Page:

Asher anokhi m'tzaveh et'khem hayom

That I command you today.

לְאַהֲבָה אֶת יְיָ אֱלֹהֵיכֶם וּלְעָבְדוֹ בְּכָל לְבַבְכֶם וּבְכָל נַפְשְׁכֶם

l'ahavah et Adonai Eloheikhem ul'av'do b'khol l'vav'khem uv'khol naf'sh'khem

to love the Lord your God and to serve him with all your heart and all your soul,

Previous Page:

l'ahavah et Adonai Eloheikhem ul'av'do b'khol l'vav'khem uv'khol naf'sh'khem

to love the Lord your God and to serve him with all your heart and all your soul,

וְנָתַתִּי מְטַר אַרְצְכֶם בְּעִתּוֹ יוֹרֶה וּמַלְקוֹשׁ
וְאָסַפְתָּ דְגָנֶךָ וְתִירֹשְׁךָ וְיִצְהָרֶךָ

V'natati m'tar ar'tz'khem b'ito yoreh umal'kosh v'asaf'ta d'ganekha v'tirosh'kha v'yitz'harekha.

That I will give rain to your land, the early and the late rains, that you may gather in your grain, your wine and your oil.

Previous Page:

V'natati m'tar ar'tz'khem b'ito yoreh umal'kosh v'asaf'ta d'ganekha v'tirosh'kha v'yitz'harekha.

That I will give rain to your land, the early and the late rains, that you may gather in your grain, your wine and your oil.

וְנָתַתִּי עֵשֶׂב בְּשָׂדְךָ לִבְהֶמְתֶּךָ וְאָכַלְתָּ וְשָׂבָעְתָּ

V'natati eisev b'sad'kha liv'hem'tekha v'akhal'ta v'sava'ta.

And I will give grass in your fields for your cattle and you will eat and you will be satisfied.

Previous Page:

V'natati eisev b'sad'kha liv'hem'tekha v'akhal'ta v'sava'ta.

And I will give grass in your fields for your cattle and you will eat and you will be satisfied.

הִשָּׁמְרוּ לָכֶם פֶּן יִפְתֶּה לְבַבְכֶם
וְסַרְתֶּם וַעֲבַדְתֶּם אֱלֹהִים אֲחֵרִים וְהִשְׁתַּחֲוִיתֶם לָהֶם

Hisham'ru lakhem pen yif'teh l'vav'khem v'sar'tem va'avad'tem Elohim acheirim v'hish'tachavitem lahem

Beware, lest your heart be deceived and you turn and serve other gods and worship them.

Previous Page:

Hisham'ru lakhem pen yif'teh l'vav'khem v'sar'tem va'avad'tem Elohim acheirim v'hish'tachavitem lahem

"Beware, lest your heart be deceived and you turn and serve other gods and worship them.

וְחָרָה אַף יְיָ בָּכֶם וְעָצַר אֶת הַשָּׁמַיִם וְלֹא יִהְיֶה מָטָר
וְהָאֲדָמָה לֹא תִתֵּן אֶת יְבוּלָהּ

V'charah af Adonai bakhem v'atzar et hashamayim v'lo yih'yeh matar v'ha'adamah lo titein et y'vulah

And anger of the Lord will blaze against you, and he will close the heavens and there will not be rain, and the earth will not give you its fullness

Previous Page:

V'charah af Adonai bakhem v'atzar et hashamayim v'lo yih'yeh matar v'ha'adamah lo titein et y'vulah

And anger of the Lord will blaze against you, and he will close the heavens and there will not be rain, and the earth will not give you its fullness

וַאֲבַדְתֶּם מְהֵרָה מֵעַל הָאָרֶץ הַטֹּבָה אֲשֶׁר יְיָ נֹתֵן לָכֶם

va'avad'tem m'heirah mei'al ha'aretz hatovah asher Adonai notein lakhem.

and you will perish quickly from the good land that the Lord gives you.

Previous Page:

va'avad'tem m'heirah mei'al ha'aretz hatovah asher Adonai notein lakhem.

and you will perish quickly from the good land that the Lord gives you.

וְשַׂמְתֶּם אֶת דְּבָרַי אֵלֶּה עַל לְבַבְכֶם וְעַל נַפְשְׁכֶם
וּקְשַׁרְתֶּם אֹתָם לְאוֹת עַל יֶדְכֶם וְהָיוּ לְטֹטָפֹת בֵּין עֵינֵיכֶם

V'sam'tem et d'varai eileh al l'vav'khem v'al naf'sh'khem uk'shar'tem otam l'ot al yed'khem v'hayu l'totafot bein eineikhem.

So you shall put these, my words, on your heart and on your soul; and you shall bind them for signs on your hands, and they shall be for frontlets between your eyes.

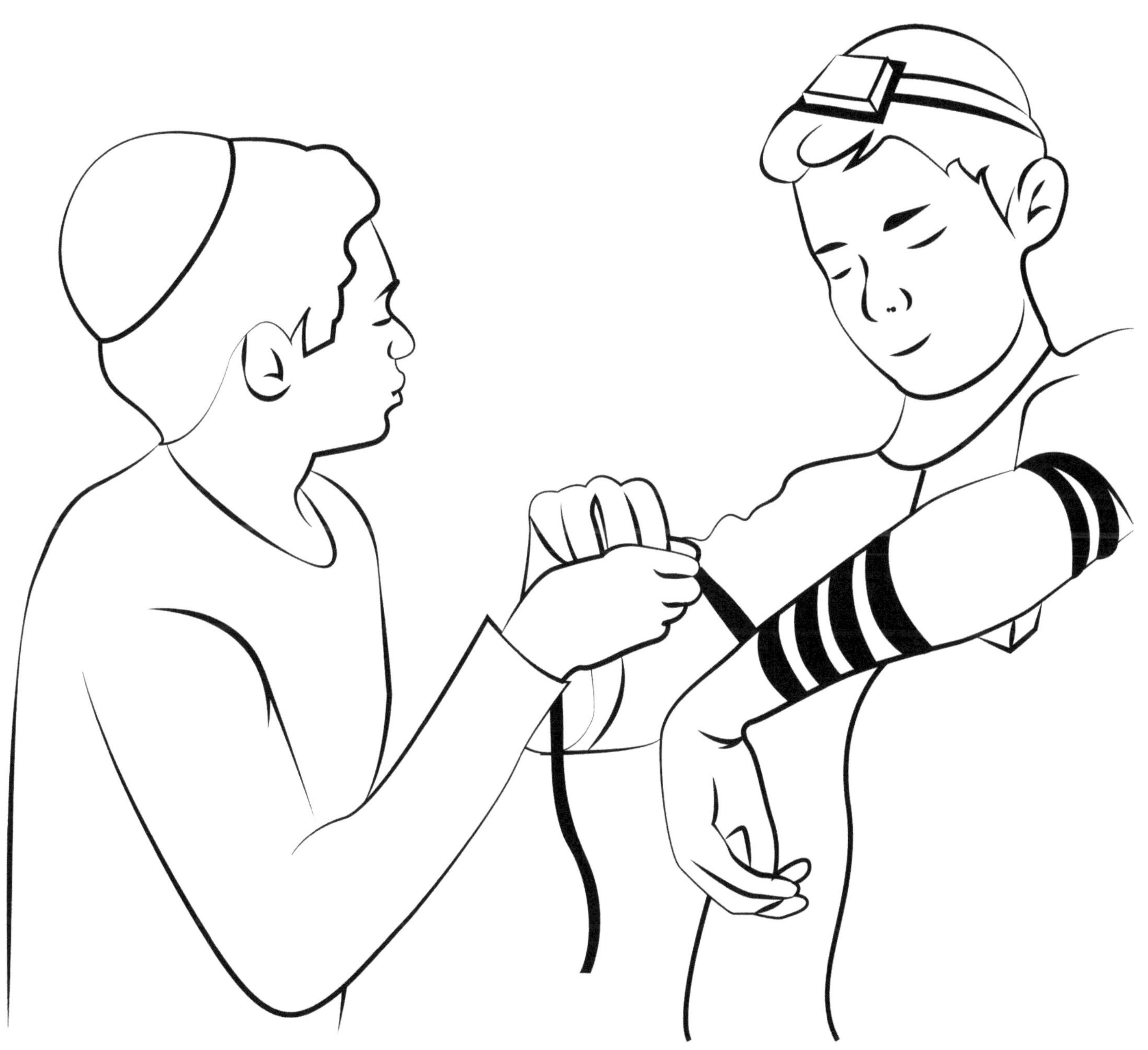

Previous Page:

V'sam'tem et d'varai elleh al l'vav'khem v'al naf'sh'khem uk'shar'tem otam l'ot al yed'khem v'hayu l'totafot bein eineikhem.

So you shall put these, my words, on your heart and on your soul; and you shall bind them for signs on your hands, and they shall be for frontlets between your eyes.

וְלִמַּדְתֶּם אֹתָם אֶת בְּנֵיכֶם לְדַבֵּר בָּם

V'limad'tem otam et b'neikhem l'dabeir bam

And you shall teach them to your children, and you shall speak of them

Previous Page:

V'limad'tem otam et b'neikhem l'dabeir bam

And you shall teach them to your children, and you shall speak of them

בְּשִׁבְתְּךָ בְּבֵיתֶךָ וּבְלֶכְתְּךָ בַדֶּרֶךְ וּבְשָׁכְבְּךָ וּבְקוּמֶךָ

b'shiv't'kha b'veitekha uv'lekh't'kha vaderekh uv'shakh'b'kha uv'kumekha

when you sit at home, and when you walk along the way, and when you lie down and when you rise up.

Previous Page:

b'shiv't'kha b'veitekha uv'lekh't'kha vaderekh uv'shakh'b'kha uv'kumekha

when you sit at home, and when you walk along the way, and when you lie down and when you rise up.

וּכְתַבְתָּם עַל מְזֻזוֹת בֵּיתֶךָ וּבִשְׁעָרֶיךָ

Ukh'tav'tam al m'zuzot beitekha uvish'arekha.

And you shall write them on the doorposts of your house and on your gates.

Previous Page:

Ukh'tav'tam al m'zuzot beitekha uvish'arekha.

And you shall write them on the doorposts of your house and on your gates.

לְמַעַן יִרְבּוּ יְמֵיכֶם וִימֵי בְנֵיכֶם עַל הָאֲדָמָה
אֲשֶׁר נִשְׁבַּע יְיָ לַאֲבֹתֵיכֶם לָתֵת לָהֶם כִּימֵי הַשָּׁמַיִם עַל הָאָרֶץ

L'ma'an yirbu y'maychem vi-y'may v'naychem al ha-adamah asher nishba Adonai la-avotaychem latayt lahem ki-y'may ha-shamayim al ha-aretz.

In order to prolong your days and the days of your children on the land that the Lord promised your fathers that he would give them, as long as the days that the heavens are over the earth.

Previous Page:

L'ma'an yirbu y'maychem vi-y'may v'naychem al ha-adamah asher nishba Adonai la-avotaychem latayt lahem ki-y'may ha-shamayim al ha-aretz.

In order to prolong your days and the days of your children on the land that the Lord promised your fathers that he would give them, as long as the days that the heavens are over the earth.

Numbers 15:37-41

וַיֹּאמֶר יְיָ אֶל מֹשֶׁה לֵּאמֹר

Vayo'mer Adonai el mosheh lei'mor

And the Lord spoke to Moses, saying...

Previous Page:

Vayo'mer Adonai el mosheh lei'mor

And the Lord spoke to Moses, saying...

דַּבֵּר אֶל בְּנֵי יִשְׂרָאֵל וְאָמַרְתָּ אֲלֵהֶם

Dabeir el b'nei Yis'ra'eil v'amar'ta aleihem

Speak to the children of Israel and say to them

Previous Page:

Dabeir el b'nei Yis'ra'eil v'amar'ta aleihem

Speak to the children of Israel and say to them

וְעָשׂוּ לָהֶם צִיצִת עַל כַּנְפֵי בִגְדֵיהֶם לְדֹרֹתָם
וְנָתְנוּ עַל צִיצִת הַכָּנָף פְּתִיל תְּכֵלֶת

v'asu lahem tzitzit al kan'fei vig'deihem l'dorotam v'nat'nu al tzitzit hakanaf p'til t'kheilet

they should make themselves tzitzit (fringes) on the corners of their clothing throughout their generations, and give the tzitzit of each corner a thread of blue.

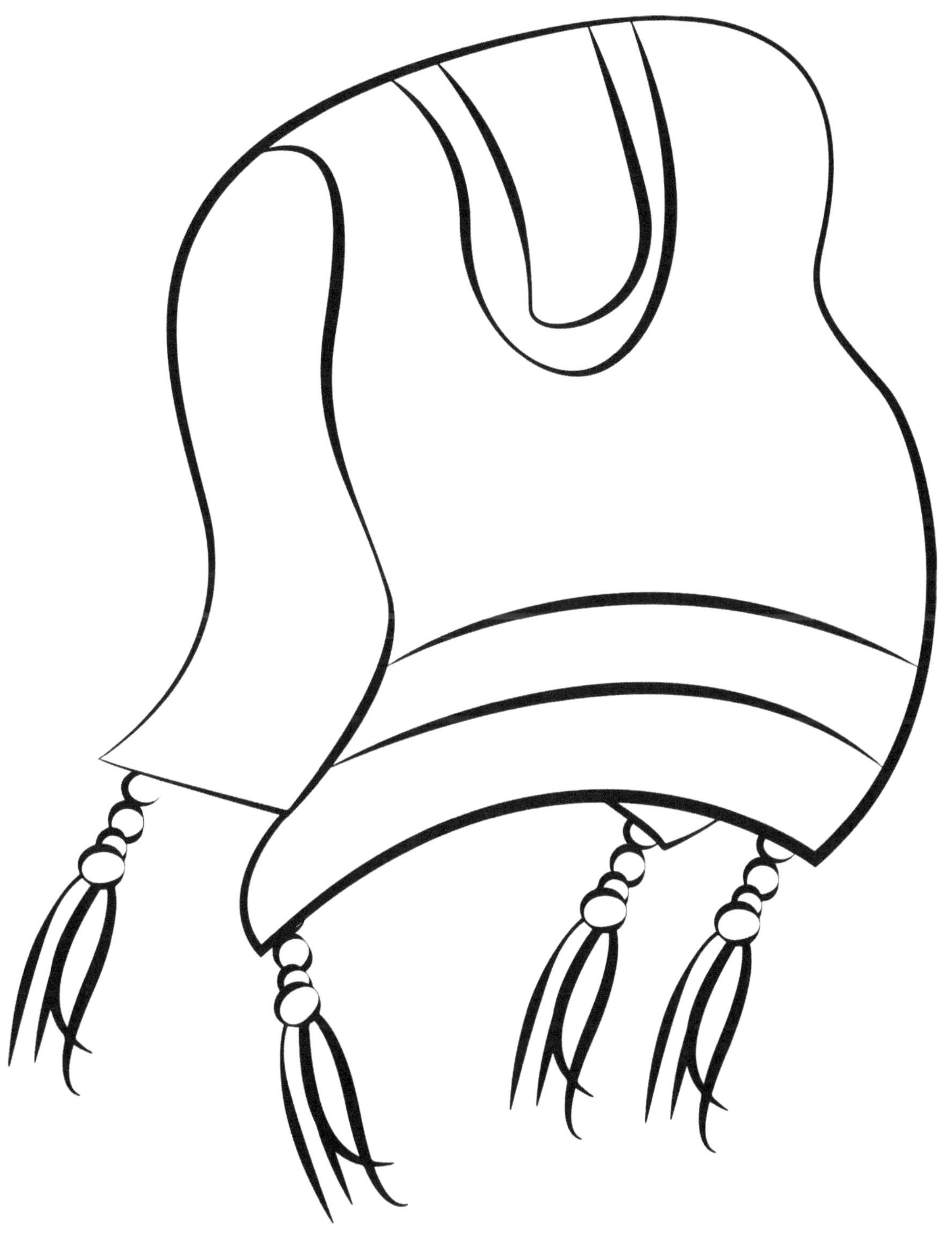

Previous Page:

v'asu lahem tzitzit al kan'fei vig'deihem l'dorotam v'nat'nu al tzitzit hakanaf p'til t'khellet

they should make themselves tzitzit (fringes) on the corners of their clothing throughout their generations, and give the tzitzit of each corner a thread of blue.

וְהָיָה לָכֶם לְצִיצִת וּרְאִיתֶם אֹתוֹ וּזְכַרְתֶּם אֶת כָּל מִצְוֹת יְיָ וַעֲשִׂיתֶם אֹתָם וְלֹא תָתוּרוּ אַחֲרֵי לְבַבְכֶם וְאַחֲרֵי עֵינֵיכֶם אֲשֶׁר אַתֶּם זֹנִים אַחֲרֵיהֶם

V'hayah lakhem l'tzitzit ur'item oto uz'khar'tem et kol mitz'vot Adonai va'asitem otam v'lo taturu acharei l'vav'khem v'acharei eineikhem asher atem zonim achareihem

And they shall be tzitzit for you, and when you look at them you will remember all of the Lord's commandments and do them and not follow after your heart and after your eyes which lead you astray.

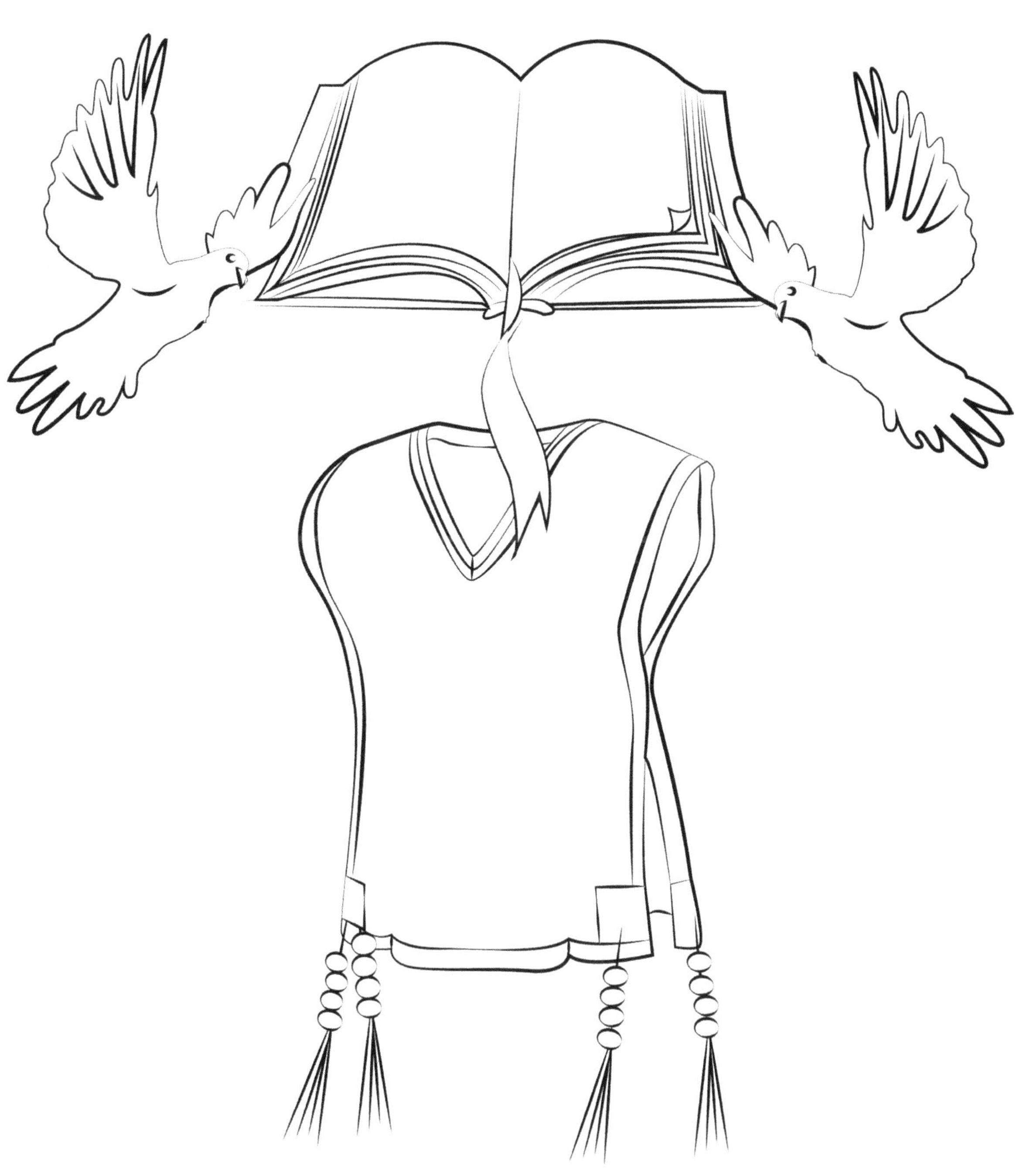

Previous Page:

V'hayah lakhem l'tzitzit ur'item oto uz'khar'tem et kol mitz'vot Adonai va'asitem otam v'lo taturu acharei l'vav'khem v'acharei eineikhem asher atem zonim achareihem

And they shall be tzitzit for you, and when you look at them you will remember all of the Lord's commandments and do them and not follow after your heart and after your eyes which lead you astray.

לְמַעַן תִּזְכְּרוּ וַעֲשִׂיתֶם אֶת כָּל מִצְוֺתָי וִהְיִיתֶם קְדֹשִׁים לֵאלֹהֵיכֶם

L'ma'an tiz'k'ru va'asitem et kol mitz'votai viyitem k'doshim lei'loheikhem

In order to remember and do all My commandments, and be holy for your God.

Previous Page:

L'ma'an tiz'k'ru va'asitem et kol mitz'votai viyitem k'doshim lel'loheikhem

In order to remember and do all My commandments, and be holy for your God.

אֲנִי יְיָ אֱלֹהֵיכֶם

Ani Adonai Eloheikhem asher hotzei'ti et'khem mei'eretz Mitz'rayim lih'yot lakhhem leilohim Ani Adonai Eloheikhem

I am the Lord, your God who lead you from the land of Egypt to be a God to you. I am the Lord, your God.

Previous Page:

Ani Adonai Eloheikhem asher hotzei'ti et'khem mel'eretz Mitz'rayim lih'yot lakhhem leilohim Ani Adonai Eloheikhem

I am the Lord, your God who lead you from the land of Egypt to be a God to you. I am the Lord, your God.

www.ingramcontent.com/pod-product-compliance
Ingram Content Group UK Ltd.
Pitfield, Milton Keynes, MK11 3LW, UK
UKHW051136260726
13967UKWH00010B/3080

9 780994 111753